The Jamestown Colony

by Brendan January

Content Adviser: Professor Sherry L. Field,
Department of Social Science Education,
College of Education, The University of Georgia

Reading Adviser: Dr. Linda D. Labbo,
Department of Reading Education,
College of Education, The University of Georgia

COMPASS POINT BOOKS

Minneapolis, Minnesota

Compass Point Books
3109 West 50th Street, #115
Minneapolis, MN 55410

Visit Compass Point Books on the Internet at *www.compasspointbooks.com* or e-mail your request
to *custserv@compasspointbooks.com*

Photographs ©: FPG International/Tom Algire, cover; Corbis/Francis G. Mayer, 4; Archive
Photos, 5, 12, 18, 22, 35; Corbis, 6; North Wind Picture Archives, 7, 16, 26, 31, 39;
Corbis/Bettmann, 8, 11 top; Unicorn Stock Photos/Dennis Mc Donald, 9; Unicorn Stock
Photos/Jeff Greenberg, 10; Corbis, 11 bottom; National Park Service, Colonial National Historical
Park, 17, 23, 29, 37; Stock Montage, Inc., 19; Photo Network/Phyllis Picardi, 21; Corbis/Roman
Soumar, 32; Corbis/Archivo Iconografico, S.A., 34; Corbis/David Muench, 41.

Editors: E. Russell Primm and Emily J. Dolbear
Photo Researcher: Svetlana Zhurkina
Photo Selector: Dawn Friedman
Design: Bradfordesign, Inc.
Cartography: XNR Productions, Inc.

Library of Congress Cataloging-in-Publication Data
January, Brendan, 1972–
   The Jamestown Colony / by Brendan F. January.
      p. cm. — (We the people)
   Includes bibliographical references and index.
   Summary: An account of the first permanent English settlement in North America, with all its
tragedies and disasters, established in 1607 in Jamestown, Virginia.
   ISBN 0-7565-0043-5 (hardcover)
   ISBN 0-7565-1023-6 (paperback)
   1. Jamestown (Va.)—History—17th century—Juvenile literature. 2. Virginia—History—
Colonial period, ca. 1600–1775—Juvenile literature. [1. Jamestown (Va.)—History. 2. Virginia—
History—Colonial period, ca. 1600–1775.] I. Title. II. We the people (Compass Point Books).
   F234.J3 J38 2000
   975.5'425101—dc21   00-008672

TABLE OF CONTENTS

FINDING AMERICA

In the late 1400s, a brave sea captain named Christopher Columbus searched for a new sea route from Europe to the Indies. The Indies included China, Japan, India, and the islands scattered around them. These lands produced tasty spices and a beautiful cloth called silk.

Christopher Columbus

In 1492, Columbus boldly sailed west across the Atlantic Ocean. He never reached the Indies. Instead, he landed at a place no living European had seen—North America.

Columbus and his crew arriving in the Americas

News of his discovery spread through Europe. Explorers from Spain, France, and England followed Columbus. In sturdy wooden ships powered by the wind, they sailed up and down North and South America. They mapped the coastline and met the people who lived there. Columbus, who believed he was in India, called the people "Indians."

South Americans at first believed the newly arrived Spanish were gods and gave them gifts.

Landing at Roanoke

In South America, the Spanish built **colonies** and found much gold and silver. The English dreamed of finding similar riches in North America. In 1587, the English established a tiny settlement on Roanoke Island, off the coast of what is now North Carolina. But the colonists suffered from a lack of food. They also were attacked by Native Americans. No one knows what happened to the colonists.

A poster advertising America

PLANNING A NEW COLONY

Despite the failure of Roanoke, a group of English **investors** planned a new colony in 1606. The group was called the London Company. To attract settlers, they wrote pamphlets about fields of gold and jewels in North America. Dreaming of easy wealth, dozens of men responded. The company chose Captain Christopher Newport to lead the voyage.

On December 20, 1606, 105 men boarded three ships near London. They were filled with food, guns, and tools. One ship, the *Susan Constant,*

The Susan Constant, *reconstructed here, was one of the ships the London Company sent to America.*

also carried a sealed metal box with instructions from the company. It was to be opened after the ships arrived in North America.

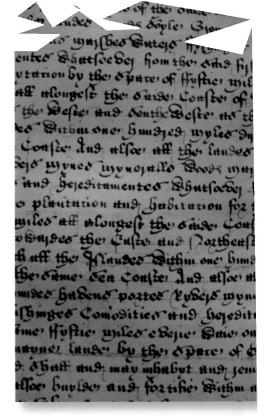

The written instructions from the London Company for establishing Jamestown

Most of the passengers called themselves gentlemen. Few had ever plowed a field or built a house. They were also very proud. When one man, John Smith, complained about the ship's leaders, they locked him up in chains.

After a long weather delay and more than three hard months at sea, they spotted land— the coast of Virginia. Excited, some of the men jumped into rowboats and went ashore.

John Smith

The first settlers arrive at Jamestown.

Native Americans watch the arrival of the English.

SWEET LAND

Vast forests stretched in every direction. In the warmth of spring, the trees and bushes sprouted new leaves. Dogwood, honeysuckle, and wild roses blossomed in brilliant colors. Fields were covered with bright-red wild strawberries. "They are four times bigger and better than ours in England," wrote one Englishman.

As they returned to their ships, Native Americans attacked the men. The Englishmen drove them off with their guns. Several Native Americans were wounded.

On the beach, Captain Newport put up a cross and thanked God for safe arrival in North America. He then opened the sealed metal box

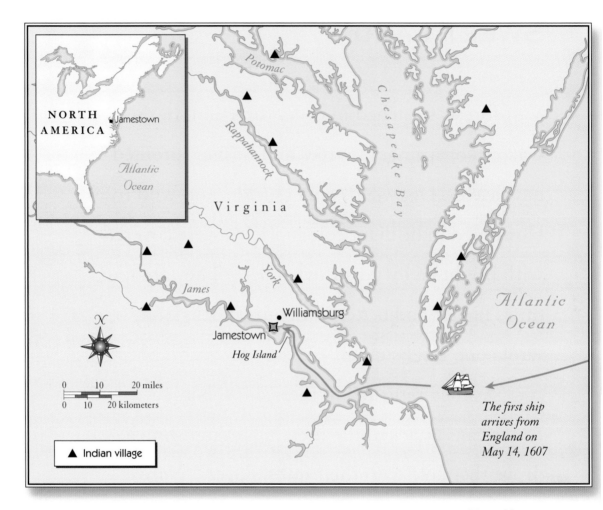

Map of Jamestown area

and read the instructions. They listed the names of seven men who would control the colony. One of them was John Smith, who was still locked up on the ship.

The instructions also ordered the company to establish a colony. The three ships sailed across the bay and found a wide river leading into Virginia. They named the river *James*, in honor of their king.

After sailing almost 30 miles (48 kilometers) up the river, Newport saw some land protected on three sides by water. The river was deep, so the ships could be tied to trees on shore. It seemed the perfect spot for a colony.

BUILDING JAMESTOWN

On May 14, 1607, the Englishmen began putting up huts and building a fort. They chopped down trees, sharpened the tops into points, and buried them in a ditch to make wooden walls.

John Smith was put in charge of the construction. The work was difficult and slow and

The English colonists build Jamestown in the wilderness.

James Fort construction, May–June, 1607

many of the men complained. But Smith, fearing an Indian attack, urged them to work quickly.

Smith's fears were correct. The fort was only half finished when Native Americans charged out of the forest. The colonists fled in confusion. One man was killed and several more were wounded. On the nearby ships, the men fired the cannon with great blasts. Scared by the booming noise, the Native Americans fled.

The settlers soon finished the fort. The fort's walls were laid out in a giant triangle. The side

James Fort

facing the James River was 420 feet (128 meters) long. The other two sides were 300 feet (92 m) each. At each corner of the fort, the settlers mounted cannon on earthen platforms. Inside the walls, they built houses, storage bins, and a church.

Yet there were problems. The tide pushed the salty ocean water upstream past the colony, making the river water undrinkable. Then clouds of buzzing mosquitoes carrying deadly diseases appeared. And the summer in Virginia was much hotter than in England. It sapped the settlers' strength.

TOUGH TIMES

As the summer grew hotter, disease spread, and many colonists died. Tired and miserable, the survivors argued. Groups of settlers ventured into the forests in search of jewels and gold. They scratched the soil with picks and shovels, hoping to find jewels. They sifted through muddy river

The colonists suffered in winter as well as summer.

bottoms for the sparkle of gold. With some excitement, they found stones that looked like gold.

On June 22, 1607, Captain Newport set sail for England with boxes of the golden rocks. Experts in London would determine if they were gold. Newport promised to return to Jamestown in a few months with more supplies.

The colonists were left with only a three-month supply of food, but no one wanted to plant crops under the broiling sun. By December 1607, only fifty colonists were still alive, and the food was almost gone.

John Smith decided to trade for food with the local Native Americans. On December 10, 1607, he and a group of men sailed up the James River. When the river narrowed, Smith pulled the boat up to a bank. He and two other men went into the forest but Native Americans soon attacked them. In the fight, two Native Americans and both of Smith's men were killed. Smith was taken prisoner.

A reconstruction of a Native American village in Jamestown

Powhatan's daughter, Pocahontas, saved Smith's life.

John Smith was taken before Powhatan, the powerful Native American leader in the area. Powhatan ordered that Smith be killed. Smith was forced to lie down on the ground with his head on a rock. A warrior was about to kill Smith by smashing his head with a club.

John Smith trading with Native Americans

At that moment, Smith wrote later, a miracle occurred. Powhatan's twelve-year-old daughter, Pocahontas, ran to Smith and took his head into her arms. Powhatan gave in to his daughter's pleas to save John Smith's life.

Later, Smith explained to Powhatan why the colonists had settled in Virginia. He told him that the English did not want to take his land. They simply wanted to trade and explore. Smith also asked for corn, and Powhatan agreed.

Smith returned to Jamestown with food and a peace agreement. In January 1608, Captain Newport returned from England with food, guns, and another 120 settlers. The colonists cheered their arrival. Only 38 of the original 105 men were still alive. Newport left again and promised to return in the summer.

JOHN SMITH'S SYSTEM

Jamestown, it seemed, had survived its first test. But the colony still faced the same problems. The new settlers didn't want to work in the fields either. They wanted to get rich and hurry back to England. "There was no talk, no hope, no work, but dig gold, wash gold, refine gold," wrote Smith with disgust.

Summer arrived with scorching heat and swarms of mosquitoes. Again, settlers grew sick and died at an alarming rate.

In October 1608, Newport arrived with more ships and more colonists, including two women. He also had new instructions from the London Company. The company leaders were unhappy that the colony was losing money. The rocks

An early map of the Jamestown settlement

Newport had brought to England were not real gold. The company ordered the colony to produce something to pay their bills.

John Smith was upset. He wrote back an

angry letter. He told the company to send colonists who knew how to work. A forceful, powerful man, Smith was elected president of the colony. He knew that the colonists needed firm rule or they would all starve. To force the colonists to work in the fields, he made a simple law: "If any would not work, neither should he eat."

Despite the colonists' grumbling, Smith's system worked. The colony grew stronger. Pigs were released on a nearby island to breed. Within a year, more than fifty pigs lived on what was named Hog Island.

The fear of starvation faded. Smith wrote that hundreds of chickens were also being raised. The nearby forest had plenty of deer, rabbits, and squirrels. And they still traded with the Native American for corn.

THE STARVING TIME

Then in August 1609, seven battered ships arrived in Jamestown. Most of the colonists were ill. Their food was rotten.

In September, John Smith was injured in a gunpowder accident. He had to return to England for treatment and never came back to Virginia.

Without Smith, the colony was in even more trouble. Food ran low and **relations** with the Native Americans fell apart. Native Americans killed thirty hungry men who ventured outside the fort.

Unable to leave the fort's walls, the starving colonists couldn't hunt or fish. Desperate, they ate dogs, cats, rats, mice, and snakes and dug up roots. One colonist wrote of "our men day and night

Burial of the dead during the Starving Time

groaning in every corner of the fort most pitiful to hear . . . some departing out of the world, many times three or four in a night; in the morning, their bodies trailed out of their cabins like dogs to be buried."

The colonists called the winter of 1609–1610 the Starving Time. Almost 500 colonists lived in Jamestown in August 1609. After that terrible winter, only 65 remained.

On May 23, 1610, two ships sailed up the James River to the colony. Shocked by the pale, bony colonists and the ragged fort, the ship commander loaded the survivors into the ships and set sail for England. The fort was left to the Native Americans and the forest.

Just a few miles downstream, however, they spotted a white sail. Three ships, loaded with equipment, settlers, and a new governor appeared on the horizon. Despite the "groans, curses, and great grief" of the surviving settlers, the ships turned back up the James River. Jamestown had been saved.

Lord De La Ware

Lord De La Ware, the new governor, took charge of the colony. He was determined not to repeat the mistakes of the past. Never again would the colonists starve during the winter. Anyone who broke the rules was whipped. All men had to work if they wanted to eat. Anyone who stole food would be punished.

For the next two years, the colony did well.

These huts are reconstructions of the original Jamestown settlement.

Settlers built houses outside the fort's walls. In August 1611, 200 men and 20 women arrived in the colony.

By now, the London Company knew that Virginia had no fields of gold. But they still demanded that the colony produce something that could make money.

A DISCOVERY

In 1612, a man named John Rolfe made an important discovery. The Native Americans grew tobacco, but Europeans had found it harsh and bitter. Rolfe planted milder tobacco seeds from the West Indies in the Virginian soil. To his delight, the golden leaves grew strong and healthy. In June 1613, Rolfe sent a ship filled with tobacco to England.

Smoking was a new habit in Europe. King James I called it hateful to the nose, harmful to the brain, and dangerous to the lungs. But most Europeans couldn't get enough of it. The Virginia tobacco sold quickly and at a great profit. In 1615, Virginia shipped 2,300 pounds (1,044 kilograms) of tobacco to England. By 1618, Virginia was

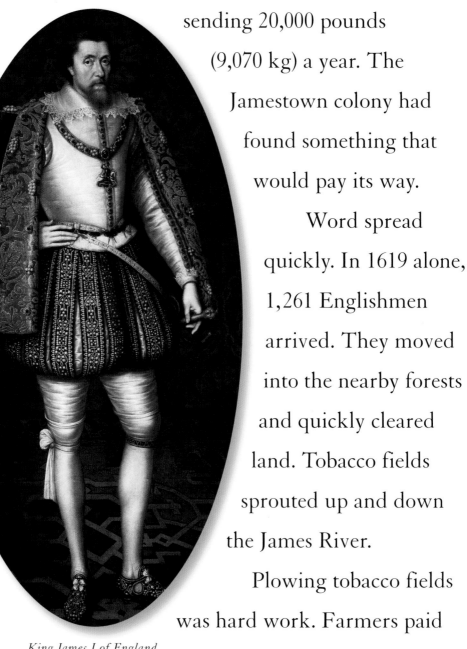

King James I of England

sending 20,000 pounds (9,070 kg) a year. The Jamestown colony had found something that would pay its way.

Word spread quickly. In 1619 alone, 1,261 Englishmen arrived. They moved into the nearby forests and quickly cleared land. Tobacco fields sprouted up and down the James River.

Plowing tobacco fields was hard work. Farmers paid

African slaves arriving in America

for poor white people to sail to Virginia and work on their plantations. After several years, these workers—called **indentured servants**—were given their freedom.

In 1619, a boat unloaded black slaves in Jamestown. White farmers bought the slaves and put them to work. For them, there would be no freedom. Slavery in English North America had begun.

The London Company also realized that the colonists would work harder if they were farming their own land. Plots of land were given to each colonist.

By 1622, the tiny, starving village on the James River had become a thriving colony. Dozens of plantations sprang up around Jamestown.

Nearby Indian tribes watched Jamestown grow with a mixture of anger and fear. Tobacco was a greedy plant that destroyed the soil after several seasons. The colonists then moved on to another area, clearing more and more woodland. They took over Indian cornfields.

Jamestown 1614, aerial view

37

A Surprise Attack

By that time, Powhatan had died. The new chief, Opechancanough, saw that the English were growing stronger and that Smith's promises had proved to be lies. The English were going to take over all the land. Opechancanough planned an attack to drive the English back into the ocean.

On March 22, 1622, Opechancanough's warriors attacked remote farms, killing the settlers and burning their buildings to the ground. Trading posts were destroyed and plantations wiped out.

Finally, Jamestown itself was attacked. After several days of battle, almost one-third of the colonists—347 settlers—were killed. But the English fought off the Indian attacks. Opechancanough's gamble had failed. Jamestown survived, and the

Opechancanough with his warriors

English declared war on all Native Americans.

Because of the Indian attack and poor colonial management, King James I took the Virginia colony from the London Company. He decided to rule it himself. The investors in the London Company lost everything.

THE END OF JAMESTOWN

Jamestown became the capital of Virginia in 1670. In 1699, when the town was damaged by fire, the government moved to a newer city called Williamsburg. The move made sense.

By 1700, Virginians were spreading west, clearing fields for farms, and building new towns. Several other colonies existed in North America— New York, Massachusetts, Pennsylvania. Within 100 years, thirteen colonies would band together and form a new country—the United States of America.

It all began at Jamestown. But by that time, the structures of Jamestown had been slowly left to the forest. The ruins of a brick church were the only evidence that a settlement had ever been there.

The rebuilt brick church at Jamestown

GLOSSARY

colonies—groups of people living in a new land with ties to a parent country; the thirteen British territories that became the original United States of America

indentured servants—people who agree to work for another person for a certain period of time in return for payment of travel and living costs

investors—people who provide money for a project in return for a share in the profits

relations—connections; the way people get along together

Did You Know?

- Jamestown's original settlers included six carpenters, two bricklayers, one barber, and one tailor.

- The Jamestown colonists ate mostly fish and turtles. They also ate birds, oysters, and raccoons as well as beef and pork they brought with them from England.

- Pocahontas married colonist John Rolfe of Jamestown in 1614.

- In 1996, archaeologists uncovered the remains of one of Virginia's first colonists. The nails and dark soil stained by rotten wood indicated the use of a coffin and the wealth of the colonist.

IMPORTANT DATES

Timeline

1606	With money from the London Company, 105 Englishmen set off to start a new colony.
1607	The colonists reach America; Pocahontas saves John Smith's life; Jamestown becomes capital of Virginia.
1608	Captain Newport returns from England.
1609–1610	More than 400 colonists die of disease and starvation.
1612	John Rolfe plants West Indian tobacco seeds in Virginian soil.
1613	Rolfe sends tobacco to England.
1619	More than 1,000 settlers arrive from England; the first black slaves are brought to Jamestown
1622	Opechancanough attacks the Jamestown colony, killing more than 300 colonists.
1699	Jamestown is damaged by fire and the government moves to Williamsburg.

IMPORTANT PEOPLE

LORD DE LA WARE
(1577–1618), *governor of Jamestown colony*

KING JAMES I
(1566–1625), *king of England*

OPECHANCANOUGH
(?–1644), *Native American chief*

POCAHONTAS
(1595–1617), *daughter of Powhatan*

POWHATAN
(1550?–1618), *Native American chief*

JOHN ROLFE
(1585–1622), *English colonist*

JOHN SMITH
(1580–1631), *English adventurer, colonist*

WANT TO KNOW MORE?

At the Library

Collier, Christopher, and James Lincoln Collier. *The Paradox of Jamestown, 1585–1700*. New York: Benchmark Books, 1998.

Fritz, Jean. *The Double Life of Pocahontas*. New York: Puffin Books, 1987.

Smith, C. Carter. *The Jamestown Colony*. Englewood Cliffs, N.J.: Silver Burdett Press, 1991.

On the Web

For more information on *The Jamestown Colony,* use FactHound to track down Web sites related to this book.

1. Go to *www.facthound.com*

2. Type in a search word related to this book or this book ID: 0756500435.

3. Click on the *Fetch It* button.

Your trusty FactHound will fetch the best Web sites for you!

Through the Mail

Jamestown-Yorktown Foundation

P.O. Box 1607

Williamsburg, VA 23187

For information about the Jamestown settlement

On the Road

Jamestown Settlement

Off of Jamestown Road

Williamsburg, VA 23185

757/253-4939

To visit replicas of the three ships that brought settlers to Virginia and re-creations of James Fort and an Indian village

INDEX

About the Author

Brendan January graduated from Haverford College and Columbia University Graduate School of Journalism. He has written several nonfiction books for young readers, including one recognized as a Best Science Book of 1999 by the National Science Teachers Association. Brendan January is currently a journalist at the *Philadelphia Inquirer* and lives with his wife in New Jersey.